CARLISLE IN 50 BUILDINGS

PAUL RABBITTS

AMBERLEY

To Julie Rabbitts, Karen Jull and Jeanette Sallie, once natives of Carlisle, also known as 'Fred, Willie and George'

First published 2022

Amberley Publishing, The Hill, Stroud
Gloucestershire GL5 4EP

www.amberley-books.com

British Library Cataloguing in Publication Data.
A catalogue record for this book is available from the British Library.

ISBN 978 1 3981 0520 1 (print)
ISBN 978 1 3981 0521 8 (ebook)

Typesetting by SJmagic DESIGN SERVICES, India.
Printed in Great Britain.

Contents

Merry Carlisle, border city,
Gallant name in tale and ditty
From the days of old;
Oft to warlike Celt and Roman,
Gentle knight and sturdy yeoman,
Was thy prowess told.

Hugh Falconer (1808–1865)

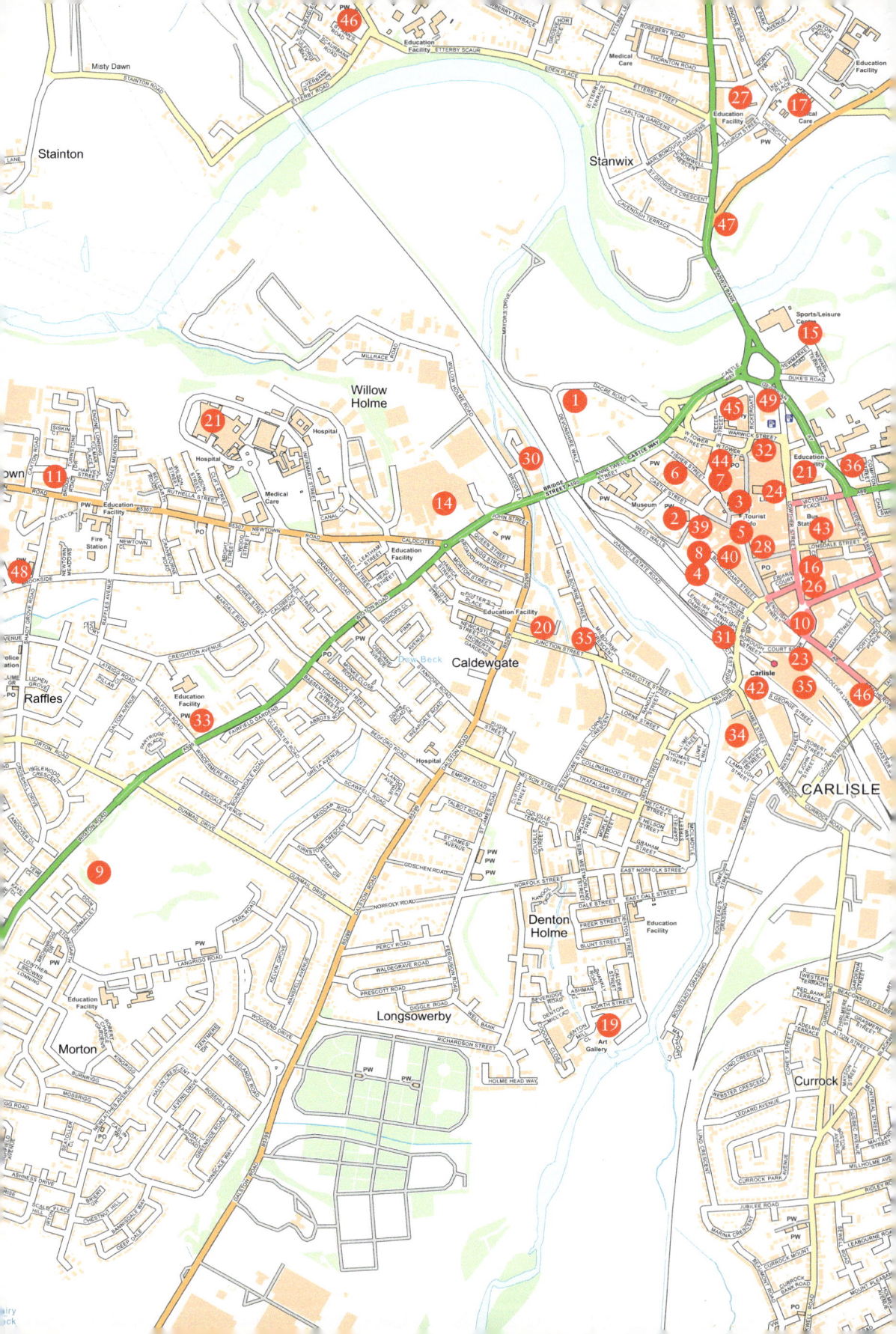

Key

1. Carlisle Castle
2. Carlisle Cathedral and Precinct
3. The Guildhall Museum
4. The Tithe Barn, West Walls
5. The Old Town Hall
6. Tullie House Museum
7. The Kings Head
8. St Cuthbert's Church
9. Morton Manor
10. Eastern and Western Towers of the Citadel
11. Coledale Hall, Newtown Road
12. Durranhill House – Sacred Heart Convent, Durranhill Road
13. Cavendish House
14. Carrs of Carlisle
15. Turf Tavern Inn
16. Lloyds Bank and The Post, Lowther Street
17. Homeacres Villa and Homeacres Cottage – Cumbria College of Art and Design
18. St John the Baptist Church, Upperby
19. Mill, Holme Head Works, Coffee Tavern and Reading Room
20. Shaddon Mill and Dixon's Chimney
21. Cumberland Infirmary and Former Carlisle Dispensary
22. The Former Garlands Hospital
23. The Former County and Station Hotel
24. The Howard Arms
25. Carlisle Citadel Railway Station
26. Congregational Church, Lowther Street
27. St Michael's Church, Stanwix
28. HSBC and Barclays Banks, English Street
29. Former Union Workhouse and City Maternity Hospital, Fusehill Street
30. Theakston's Carlisle Brewery
31. Viaduct House, Victoria Viaduct
32. The Market Hall and Covered Market
33. Church of Our Lady and St Joseph, Warwick Square and St Bede's, Wigton Road
34. Hudson Scotts, Carlisle Enterprise Centre and the former Electric Lighting Station Building
35. Carlisle Christian Fellowship, Charlotte Street
36. Carliol Building Trinity School
37. Red Gables
38. St Aidan's Church
39. The Crown and Mitre Hotel
40. House of Fraser Store
41. Brunton Park, Warwick Road
42. Turkish Baths, James Street
43. Former Crown Post Office, Warwick Road
44. Central Methodist Hall, Fisher Street
45. Former Fire and Police Headquarters, Rickergate
46. Carlisle Public Houses by Harry Redfern
47. Eden Bridge Gardens Rest Rooms
48. St Barnabas Church
49. Civic Centre, Rickergate
50. Cumbria County Council Offices, Botchergate

Introduction

Carlisle is the city and the county town of Cumbria. It is located at the confluence of the rivers Eden, Caldew and Petteril, 10 miles south of the Scottish border. It is the largest settlement in the county of Cumbria and serves as the administrative centre for both Carlisle City Council and Cumbria County Council. At the time of the 2001 census, the population of Carlisle was 100,734. Twenty years later, at the 2021 census, the city's population had risen to 108,000.

The early history of Carlisle is marked by its status as a Roman settlement, established to serve the forts on Hadrian's Wall. During the Middle Ages, because of its proximity to the kingdom of Scotland, Carlisle became an important military stronghold; Carlisle Castle, still relatively intact, was built in 1092 by William Rufus, and once served as a prison for Mary, Queen of Scots. The castle now houses the Duke of Lancaster's Regiment and the Border Regiment Museum. In the early twelfth century, Henry I allowed the foundation of a priory in Carlisle.

Colville Street, Denton Holme, with Dixon's Chimney in the background. The author lived here behind the blue door. Nothing has changed.

The town gained the status of a city when its diocese was formed in 1133, and the priory became Carlisle Cathedral.

The introduction of textile manufacturing during the Industrial Revolution began a process of socio-economic transformation in Carlisle, which developed into a densely populated mill town. This, combined with its strategic position, allowed for the development of Carlisle as an important railway town, with seven railway companies sharing Carlisle railway station.

Nicknamed 'the Great Border City', Carlisle today is the main cultural, commercial and industrial centre for north Cumbria. It is home to the main campuses of the University of Cumbria and a variety of museums and heritage centres. The former county borough of Carlisle had held city status until the Local Government Act 1972 was enacted in 1974. This book is therefore a celebration of the architecture that has shaped this city and was a joy to do, the author having lived here for many years between 1992 and 2000 when he called it 'home'.

English Street, and a view that has changed very little.

The 50 Buildings

1. Carlisle Castle

Carlisle Castle was first built during the reign of William II of England, the son of William the Conqueror who invaded England in 1066. At that time, Cumberland was still considered a part of Scotland. William II ordered the construction of a Norman-style motte-and-bailey castle in Carlisle on the site of an old Roman fort, with construction beginning in 1093. The need for a castle in Carlisle was to keep the northern border of England secured against the threat of invasion from Scotland. In 1122, Henry I of England ordered a stone castle to be constructed on the site.

The act of driving out the Scots from Cumberland led to many attempts to retake the lands. The result of this was that Carlisle and its castle would change hands many times for the next 700 years. The first attempt began during the troubled reign of Stephen of England. On the 26 March 1296, John 'The Red' Comyn, since the fourth quarter of 1295 Lord of Annandale, led a Scottish host across the Solway to attack Carlisle. The then governor of the castle, one Robert de Brus, deposed Lord of Annandale, successfully withstood the attack, before forcing the raiders to retreat back through Annandale to Sweetheart Abbey. From the mid-thirteenth century until the unification of England and Scotland in 1603, Carlisle Castle was the vital headquarters of the Western March, a buffer zone to protect the western portion of the Anglo-Scottish border.

Henry VIII converted the castle for artillery, employing the engineer Stefan von Haschenperg. For a few months in 1567, Mary, Queen of Scots was imprisoned within the castle – in the Warden's Tower, which was demolished in 1835. Later, the castle was besieged by the Parliamentary forces for eight months in 1644, during the English Civil War. The most important battles for the city of Carlisle and its castle were during the second Jacobite rising against George II of Great Britain in 1745. The forces of Prince Charles Edward Stuart travelled south from Scotland into England, reaching as far south as Derby. Carlisle and the castle were seized and fortified by the Jacobites. However, they were driven north by the forces of William Augustus, Duke of Cumberland, the son of George II. Carlisle was recaptured, and the Jacobites were jailed and executed. That battle marked the end of the castle's fighting life, as defending the border between England and Scotland was not necessary with both countries again part of Great Britain. After 1746, the castle became somewhat neglected, although some minor repairs were undertaken such as that of the drawbridge in 1783.

Above: Carlisle Castle and its main entrance. (© Ben Abel)

Left: The main keep of the castle. (© Ben Abel)

Some parts of the castle were then demolished for use as raw materials in the nineteenth century to create more or less what is visible to the visitor today. The army eventually moved in to take hold of the castle and in 1873 a system of recruiting areas based on counties was instituted under the Cardwell Reforms and the castle became the depot for the 34th (Cumberland) Regiment of Foot and the 55th (Westmorland) Regiment of Foot. Under the Childers Reforms, the 34th and 55th regiments amalgamated to form the Border Regiment with its depot in the castle in 1881. The castle remained the depot of the Border Regiment until 1959, when the regiment amalgamated with the King's Own Royal Regiment (Lancaster) to form the King's Own Royal Border Regiment.

2. Carlisle Cathedral and Precinct

Carlisle Cathedral was begun in 1122, during the reign of King Henry I. Many large churches of Augustinian foundation were built in England during this period as the Archbishop of Canterbury, William de Corbeil, was a member of this order, but Carlisle is one of only four Augustinian churches in England to become a cathedral, most monastic cathedrals being Benedictine. The church was begun by Athelwold, an Englishman, who became the first prior. In 1133, the church was raised to the status of cathedral and Athelwold became the first Bishop of Carlisle. In 1233, the cathedral priory community were joined by two friaries in the city. A Dominican friary and a Franciscan friary were founded close to the cathedral. The building was refurbished in the thirteenth and fourteenth centuries, receiving impetus from the presence of the court of Edward I in 1307.

In the fifteenth and early sixteenth centuries, the monastic buildings were renewed. With the Dissolution of the Monasteries from 1536, and the establishment by Henry VIII of the Church of England as the country's official church, the Dominican and Franciscan friaries were dissolved and Carlisle, along with the other monastic cathedrals, was run by a secular chapter like the cathedrals at Lincoln and York, which practice has continued to this day. During the time of the English Civil War, a portion of the nave of the cathedral was demolished by the Scottish Presbyterian Army in order to use the stone to reinforce Carlisle Castle. Between 1853 and 1870 Carlisle Cathedral was restored by Ewan Christian.

The choir is roofed by a fine wooden barrel vault dating from the fourteenth century. In 1856, this was restored and repainted to a new design by Owen Jones. The most significant architectural feature of Carlisle Cathedral is its east window. The tracery of this window is in the most complex of English Gothic styles, Flowing Decorated Gothic. It is the largest and most complex such window in England, being 51 feet high and 26 feet wide.

Within the precinct of the cathedral are found some of the finest and oldest buildings in Carlisle. In medieval times the fratry building was the dining hall of the cathedral priory. Over the intervening 800 or so years it has been used as a kitchen, a place of worship, an arsenal for the King's Army, a Civil War storeroom, a chapter house, a brewery and granary, a barn and a library. In 2020, a major project was completed that aimed to bring this hugely underused building back to life, with a world-class education and events space at the heart of the cathedral precinct. The fratry and undercroft is now a cultural hub and Carlisle's newest-oldest exhibition and events space, with a brand-new café and meeting point created alongside.

Also within the grounds of Carlisle Cathedral is the deanery, with its fourteenth-century 'pele' tower, called the Prior's Tower, which contains a fine, painted sixteenth-century heraldic ceiling. The present tower was built in the fifteenth century. It was just inside the ancient walls of the city of Carlisle, and so provided both a useful lookout and a place of safety during Scottish raids. The ground floor, or undercroft, with its thick walls, was used as a storeroom for such things as food, ale and wine. The first-floor room is known as the 'Prior's Room'. Here the prior of the monastery had his day room. It is a well-built room with double walls and a passage between them. Originally the stone walls and small windows would have made this an austere living room, office and meeting room for the head of the monastery. It was at the time of Prior Senhouse (1505–20) that the fireplace was built and the ceiling painted. The design of the ceiling consists of three themes – the Senhouse crest, various scrolls and a section incorporating the scallop of the Dacre family and the tree of the Greystoke family. The second floor was the prior's bedroom, with undecorated walls, traces of a fireplace and a 'garderobe' (or en-suite loo). This room now houses the Angela Bevan collection of dolls. These were presented to the cathedral in 1995, and the collection consists of dolls representing the kings and queens of England from William Rufus to the present royal family.

Carlisle Cathedral from the deanery.

Above: Carlisle Cathedral, resplendent in the winter sunshine, and a major tourist attraction for the city today.

Below: Carlisle Cathedral, built in local red sandstone, has been restored on many occasions.

Above: The fratry building was once the dining hall of the cathedral priory.

Below: The fratry and undercroft is now a cultural hub and Carlisle's newest-oldest exhibition and events space, with a brand-new café and meeting point created alongside.

Above: Abbey Gate. Entrance to the cathedral precinct from Abbey Street. with Tullie House visible just through the archway.

Right: The deanery within the cathedral grounds, with its fourteenth-century 'pele' tower, known as the Prior's Tower.

3. The Guildhall Museum

The Redness Hall, or the Guildhall building, is believed to date from the late fourteenth century. It takes its earlier name from a merchant, Richard de Redness, to whom it belonged between 1377 and 1399. For centuries it was the meeting place of the eight trade guilds of the city. These guilds were the Merchants, Smiths, Weavers, Tailors, Butchers, Shoemakers, Skinners and Glovers, and Tanners. The principal business of the guild meetings seems to have been dining and drinking together. Items of plate were frequently given by wealthy landowners or merchants who sought to curry favour with the guilds.

The building is characterised with its upper floors projecting out in the usual fashion of timber-framed structures. The building was extensively renovated in 1978–79, but much early timber work survives, as do wattle-and-daub internal walls.

The ground floor of the building is now occupied by a private business. There is no evidence that this was ever an open structure; it seems to have functioned for various types of trading from at least the sixteenth century, and possibly throughout its existence. The present museum entrance and staircase are of relatively modern date and the upper floors were probably accessed originally from Fisher Street. The open roof structure shows two markedly dissimilar types of construction, although research has revealed that all the timber dates from the

The Guildhall, one of the oldest buildings in the city.

time the building was originally constructed. There is virtually no documentary evidence of the construction or early structure of the Guildhall, and the earliest illustrations are of nineteenth century date. Today, the Guildhall is a Grade I Ancient Monument, and one of the four oldest buildings in the city.

4. The Tithe Barn, West Walls

The Tithe Barn stands just off the West Wall, near to St Cuthbert's Church. It was built by Prior Gondibour between 1484 and 1507 for storage of the tithes in kind collected by the church. It consists of one long chamber around 120 feet long and 24 feet wide, with walls 3 feet, 7 inches thick. At the foot of the city wall opposite, down what is called Sallyport, there used to be a small doorway with steps leading up to the wall close to the barn. This may have been used by the scouts and sortie parties when the city was besieged, or it may equally well have been for the convenience of getting the produce into the barn without it passing through one of the gates and being subject to taxes.

It has had a complicated history since then, functioning as a barn until the Dissolution of the Monasteries by Henry VIII, and then as a stable, dispensary, dwelling house and joiner's shop. Semi-derelict by 1970, it was purchased and restored by St Cuthbert's Church and has been used as a church hall since then.

The Tithe Barn, tucked away on the West Walls.

5. The Old Town Hall

The earliest reference to the predecessor of this building was in 1345, variously termed the 'Toll booth', 'Common Hall' and 'Motehall' or 'Moot Hall' in later medieval sources. In 1668, the medieval hall was demolished to make way for a new one on the same site. It is this building, finished in 1669, with numerous subsequent alterations and extensions, which survives today.

Above: The Old Town Hall, finished in 1669, had countless alterations over the years.

Left: The Old Town Hall roof's clock and bell. (©Arthur 'Pensioner' Percy)

Over the years, the ground floor of the building has consistently remained in commercial and retail use while the grander public rooms at first-floor level have accommodated a number of important civic functions, including most notably the Courts of Assize until 1881, the City's Magistrates Court until 1941, and Council Chamber and offices of the City of Carlisle Corporation until 1964. Robert Burns visited Carlisle in 1787. He stayed at the Malt Shovel Inn in Rickergate, and was fined by the mayor in the Town Hall for allowing his horse, Jenny Geddes, to trespass on corporation grass. As he departed the poet is reputed to have turned in his saddle saying, 'Come on my lass, ye'll be a mare when he's nae mair'. Poetic indeed.

The first floor now accommodates the Tourist Information Centre and Assembly Room. Essential repair work was completed both internally and externally at the start of July 2013 to ensure this historic building remains in the best possible condition.

6. Tullie House Museum

By the end of the eighteenth century there were already two museums in Cumbria which were open to the public, although both were privately owned. It was not until 1834 that the Carlisle Literary and Philosophical Society formed their first museum. This lasted for only 10 years, after which its collections were put into store, later to form the basis of the first public museum in Carlisle, which opened in 1877 in the Old Academy of Arts, Finkle Street. The collections rapidly increased and soon the old building, which had only two or three rooms, was bursting at the seams. When Tullie House came up for sale in 1890, a public subscription was raised to secure it for the city as a site for a museum, art gallery, library and centre for the study of art and sciences. As part of the change of use as a cultural centre, new extensions were built to the designs of J. Ferguson, with the whole complex opening on 8 November 1893.

The name of Tullie House is derived from the original owner, Thomas Tullie, who had the house constructed in 1689, the date can still be seen on the ornate leaden down-spouts. This is the only house of this date and style to survive in Carlisle and it is a particularly fine example of Jacobean architecture. Relatives of the Tullie family occupied the house until 1817 when it was sold to Col. Salkeld for £5,000. It remained in private hands until 1871, the last occupants being the Dixons, when part of the building was converted into a drapery warehouse. By 1890 Tullie House was in such a dilapidated state that there was talk of demolition, but fortunately it was spared this fate and now forms part of the buildings complex housing Carlisle's now famous museum and art gallery. The historic buildings are Grade I listed. A new range of buildings was added in 1989–90 to create new galleries and related facilities. This extended the site considerably on the north and east sides. Controversially, the last development (2000–01) created the Carlisle Millennium Gallery, which extends below the A595 road on the north side of the site. A public walkway connecting Castle Street to the Castle Green, runs alongside this and was also controversial at the time, the original scheme including a number of glass pyramids, which were eventually dropped.

Above: Tullie House Museum and the restored herb garden.

Left: A Grade I listed building with its ornate leaden down-spouts.

Right: The main entrance to Tullie House from Castle Street.

Below: The Millennium Gallery and new entrance was so controversial that the ruling Labour-controlled city council lost control to the Conservatives while the rest of the country was turning Labour – an example of local issues affecting local politics.

7. The Kings Head

The Kings Head is situated in the heart of the town centre behind the Town Hall and opposite the Guildhall. Along with The Sportsman and The Joiners Arms, the Kings Head is one the oldest pubs in the city. The present building dates from the seventeenth century but it is understood to be on a site occupied by a hostelry as far back as the tenth century. The Kings Head first appears in the Parson & White directory of 1829, the proprietor then being a Mr James Sawyer, who was a veteran of the Peninsular War and the Battle of Waterloo.

During the First World War, thousands of workers were drafted in to build and work for the massive munitions depot at Gretna. The growth of drunkenness was gradual at first but by the spring of 1916, disorder had spread to such an extent as to threaten and undermine the ordinary social life of the city. Lloyd George, fearing riots would take place, as in Ireland at the time, introduced the Liquor Control Board. This scheme was thought to be temporary and become known as the Carlisle Experiment, but it was to last fifty-five years. In October 1916, the

The Kings Head on the corner of Rosemary Lane.

running of The Kings Head was taken over by the said Liquor Control Board. With the Licensing Act of 1921 the Control Board was abolished and the Carlisle and District State Management Scheme evolved to take over the city's pubs, the Kings Head being acquired by the State Management in 1922. On 25 May 1971, a bill to abolish the State Management Scheme was presented to Parliament. The move was generally welcomed. In early 1971 the State Management began selling off the county pubs, The Kings Head being acquired by John Smiths on 7 May 1973. In 1984, it was sold once again, at which time the premises were extensively redecorated.

8. St Cuthbert's Church

The original St Cuthbert's Church is believed to have been erected shortly after the saint's visit to the city in AD 686. It is supposed that at the time there was a monastery at or near Carlisle fit to receive Queen Earmenburge, who was staying in Carlisle while her husband, King Ecgfrith, was fighting the Scots. It was so completely destroyed by the Danes in the ninth century that William Rufus found it to be a mere heap of ruins, taken over by great oak trees. The church was rebuilt around this time, for in 1133 the two ancient parishes of St Cuthbert and St Mary were in existence. During the Civil War it was the intention, fortunately not

St Cuthbert's Church and the picturesque churchyard just off the city centre.

realised of the Parliamentary leaders, to leave St Cuthbert's as the only church in Carlisle, and around this time the mayor and Corporation shifted their pew from St Mary's to St Cuthbert's. The steeple had been taken down towards the end of Elizabeth's reign, and in 1702 Bishop Nicolson gives a very uninviting description of the church. It was pulled down and the present building erected in 1778. All that remains of the older buildings is a fourteenth-century stained-glass window. One extremely unusual feature is the pulpit, moveable on rails, and very tall so that the vicar could preach to the galleries. Today there are more churches and holy wells in Cumbria dedicated to St Cuthbert than to any other saint.

9. Morton Manor

Morton Manor is an early nineteenth-century building, replacing an earlier farmhouse, which has been used as the Morton Community Centre since 1967. The house and surrounding park were given to the people of Carlisle by

Morton Manor, now a community centre, but once the home of Sir Robert Chance.

Morton Manor and its grand entrance and porch.

Sir Robert Chance, whose family lived there for many years. The original house was built just after 1807 for the Forsters, who had banking interests in the city. In 1853, it was bought by Joseph Ferguson, a local textile manufacturer, and when he died he left it to the Chances, who were nephews. Frederick Chance lived here and left it to Robert Chance, who lived here until 1960. He was an industrialist and prominent citizen who died in 1960. In front of the house is a rather fine example of a ha-ha, a ditch built to keep grazing animals out of the garden. The manor itself has a rich history, originally being built as a family home of the local mill owners, the Ferguson family. Originally designed by William Sawrey Gilpin, the impressive surrounding gardens, now known as Chances Park, is a haven for local people and wildlife. The manor has a projecting central ashlar porch and has engaged Ionic columns, double panelled doors in stone architrave under the Chance family motto 'DEO NON FORTUNA'.

10. Eastern and Western Towers of the Citadel

Few people who now pass between these two round towers, today known as the Citadel, realise that they are a tribute to the advance of the power of artillery. Almost 500 years after the castle and walls were erected, it was realised that sixteenth-century military tactics rendered the castle less impregnable than had been thought. Cromwell was advised in 1539 of the necessity of a citadel

The Court Houses, taken from the railway station, and a busy Edwardian scene.

C 1387 Court Houses, Carlisle.

within the town, and in 1541 Henry VIII had the castle strengthened and also ordered the construction of a second fortress in case the castle was overpowered. From 1541 to 1543, the work was entrusted to Stefan von Haschenperg, the 'gentleman of Moravia', whose first job in England was at Sandgate Castle in Kent. Little is known of this fellow apart from that much later he was accused of misappropriating quite a sum of the king's money. Originally, this defensible entrance would have consisted of two massive stone-built towers, with a U-shaped bastion behind it. On the west side of these structures was the ancient English Gate, and in the centre was the Botchard Gate (which gives its name to the present road, Botchergate). On both the east and west sides of this structure, huge triangular artillery platforms were constructed, capable of housing cannon, with the round towers providing more defensive capabilities against any would-be attackers. The walls were probably around 3 metres thick, reflecting the need for walls capable of holding heavy artillery, and withstanding any artillery attack on the southernmost part of the city's defences.

In 1807, as there was no other building convenient for holding assizes and quarter sessions, an Act was passed granting the Citadel and adjoining ground for the building of courts of justice for the county. As a result, the towers and turret were demolished.

These days, of the two original towers, only the eastern tower has any original surviving masonry. An excellent recreation of the western tower was erected on the site of the original during the period 1810 to 1817. This tower was designed by architect Sir Robert Smirke, who did extensive work on Lowther Castle, and was

The eastern tower of the Citadel, designed by Thomas Telford and Sir Robert Smirke.

intended to be as similar to the original mid-sixteenth-century tower as possible. This tower housed the assize courts.

The eastern tower, with some original masonry, was designed by Thomas Telford and Sir Robert Smirke. During renovation work conducted in the 1980s much of the original sixteenth-century external stone was replaced, thus making the two towers look as if they are of the same period.

Right: Both towers of the Citadel, with little remaining of the original buildings.

Below: The Courts buildings behind the Citadel Towers.

Coledale Hall, a fine example of Cumbrian architecture.

11. Coledale Hall, Newtown Road

Bow windows, a cornice, a parapet and a gabled porch all come together to make Coledale Hall a standout piece of Cumbrian architecture. Dating from 1810, it was the home of Henry Fawcett, Member of Parliament for Carlisle, and consisted of a house and stable range, eventually becoming a house and office. Records show alterations in 1846 for George Mould, a railway contractor. In 1926, it became St Mary's Home for Friendless Girls, and eventually a Health Authority Office. The house name comes from Richard Coledale, a merchant who lived here in the reign of Henry VI.

12. Durranhill House – Sacred Heart Convent, Durranhill Road

The building once known as Durranhill House was formerly the home of the Sacred Heart Convent, but was also at one time the home of the Lowry family. The Lowry family were of 'Durnhill' well before the present house was built. An unexecuted design for the house of Richard Lowry exists, but the present house dates from 1811. Richard Lowry died in a fall from his horse in 1841,

Once a convent, now residential.

The former chapel, converted into a residential property.

aged sixty-six, and is buried in Wetheral graveyard. The house was then let by his daughter to various tenants. The eventual sale of the house to an order of nuns is recorded in *Carlisle Journal* in 1906. Today, the building has been restored and is now residential, along with its adjacent chapel.

13. Cavendish House

Cavendish House is located at No. 83 Warwick Road and was built for Revd Thomas Woodrow, grandfather of President Wilson, the 28th President of the United States. Thomas Woodrow was originally from Paisley, and was minister at the Congregational Church on Annetwell Street from 1820. As the family grew in size he needed a larger house and had one built on Warwick Road. He returned to Scotland in 1835, leaving a brother in Carlisle and it was from Glasgow that he emigrated with his family to the USA. His wife died in 1836 from an illness

Cavendish House, with more than significant American interest.

that developed on the voyage, but the children survived. After a brief spell in Canada, the family settled in Ohio where Thomas Woodrow was pastor at the First Presbyterian Church, Chillicothe. One of his daughters, Janet, who was born in Carlisle, met a prominent journalist and politician, Joseph Ruggles Wilson, who she married in 1849. He became pastor at Staunton, Virginia, where their son Thomas Woodrow Wilson was born on 28 December 1856. After studying law at university he went on to be a teacher, but was drawn into politics, successfully standing as the Democratic presidential candidate in 1912, to become the president of the USA. President Wilson was to eventually make a visit to Carlisle on 29 December 1918.

14. Carrs of Carlisle

Carr & Co. Ltd have been making biscuits in Carlisle since 1832 when Jonathan Dodgson Carr of Kendal built the flower mill, bakery and a shop on Castle Street in which he sold hand-made biscuits. By 1834 he had moved to larger premises in Caldewgate. He was the first biscuit maker to be honoured by royal appointment to Her Majesty Queen Victoria in 1841, and the company continued to hold appointments from each succeeding sovereign to this day. Carrs was to become one of the most best-known biscuit manufacturers in the Commonwealth.

Carr himself was a Quaker and supported the temperance movement and was responsible for the Temperance Hall opposite the factory in 1861, to provide recreation and reading rooms. He was also responsible for building a school and houses for his workers in Kendal Street and Silloth Street.

The Caldewgate factory expanded to become a substantial complex with a bakery on the one side of the road and a corn mill in Denton Holme. The corn

Above: Carlisle is well known for a number of national brands, McVitie's being one of the most renowned.

Right: Carr & Co. Ltd, biscuit manufacturers.

mill was eventually relocated to Silloth. Carrs is now part of United Biscuits and has continued to expand in this location and is one of Carlisle's most famous 'brands'.

15. Turf Tavern Inn

Horse racing on the Swifts dates from the mid-sixteenth century. The course was bounded on the west, north and east by the River Eden and to the south by what became Strand Road. Racing continued here until 1904, when it transferred to the present site at Blackwell. A reminder of this past use is one of the more unusual buildings that remains in the city: the former grandstand hotel, the Turf Tavern Inn, which overlooked the racecourse on the Swifts. Built between 1839 and 1840 for the racecourse shareholders, it was extended in 1874 by Daniel Birkett. It is built of snecked calciferous sandstone ashlar with patterned cast-iron parapet railings that were added to prevent anyone falling off. With its sloping graduated local slate roof, this was formerly stepped as a grandstand, hence the central

Above: The Turf Tavern, once connected to horse racing on the Swifts.

Left: The former grandstand has long since disappeared, although the railings remain.

access. The *Carlisle Journal* stated in 1840 that the building was almost complete. When the racecourse closed in 1904, the building continued as a public house with a bowling green on the original paddock – now the car park. The building was purchased from the State Control Board in 1972 and left unoccupied and in a ruinous state until it was renovated in 1988 and became the Turf Tavern.

16. Lloyds Bank and The Post, Lowther Street

What is now Lloyds Bank was originally Carlisle's principal post office, which moved to new premises on the Warwick Road in 1916. This particular building seems to have been completed around 1840, as the OS map of the period shows the site occupied by the 'Athenaeum', with the post office to the right. The Athenaeum opened on 28 April 1840. It was originally equipped with a lecture theatre, museum, exhibition and concert rooms, and housed the Mechanics' Institution. Designed by Arthur and George Williams of Liverpool, it contained a large lecture room capable of seating 1,000 people and was until 1851 the home of the Mechanics' Institute and Library.

The 'Athenaeum' was purchased by the Post Office in 1874. Period OS maps show no evidence of any of these premises being a pub prior to 1916. But the

Lowther Street has some of the finest buildings in Carlisle, with the former Athenaeum central to an outstanding streetscape.

An eclectic mix of architecture, with the former Athenaeum, post office and existing Congregational Church.

Below left: The former post office, now a popular restaurant in the city.

Below right: The Grade II listed building at No. 22 Lowther Street.

Above: In 1868 and 1881 occupied by Hope and Bendal, wine and spirit merchants.

Right: Not every building on Lowther Street is joyful.

1925 OS map shows the entire site – from the turreted building to the building with the blinds – as the 'Gretna Tavern'.

The central section (now Lloyds Bank) was sold to the Trustee Saving Bank between 1925 and 1938 leaving the two flanking buildings plus an adjoining section behind the bank building as the 'Gretna Tavern'.

Today, the building on the left is commercial premises while the central section is a branch of Lloyds Bank. Only the original post office to the far right are licensed premises – now a restaurant.

17. Homeacres Villa and Homeacres Cottage – Cumbria College of Art and Design

Built in the late 1840s or early 1850s, Homeacres is now part of the University of Cumbria. When built this was called The Villa and is marked as such on the 1865 OS map; later it was known as Stanwix Villa. J. D. Carr lived here between 1845 and 1854, and it may have been built for him. It appears the name was changed by James Morton when he came to live here in 1900. The house was eventually

Above: Tucked away off Brampton Road is Homeacres Villa and its cottage, which are now part of the University of Cumbria.

Left: Homeacres Cottage, once lived in by George Head Head of Rickerby.

Once Cumbria College of Art and Design, now part of the growing complex that is the University of Cumbria.

compulsorily purchased by the city council in 1949 and it became the College of Art in 1951. Nearby is Homeacres Cottage, built in 1854 for George Head Head of Rickerby. This was built as the Cumberland Reformatory for boys and today forms part of the university.

18. St John the Baptist Church, Upperby

The church of St John the Baptist, understood to have been built in 1839 and opened 1840 in early Gothic Revival style, has a church tower and exposed roof structure practically identical to those of the church of St John the Evangelist, in nearby Houghton. The principal characteristic of both church towers is the bold short conical pinnacles with fleur-de-lis finials and corbelled castellated parapet. Also, as at Houghton, the corner buttresses to the nave have similar pinnacles and a simple stone cross terminates the gable over the chancel arch. The similarities are so marked that it must be assumed that both churches are the work of the same architect. To the west end the entrance to the nave is through a Tudor arched opening also reminiscent of details at Houghton. Upperby became part of the city in 1912, but when the church was built, was part of one of the many villages that became engulfed into the growing conurbation.

The Gothic Revival style of Upperby's most well-known church.

19. Mill, Holme Head Works, Coffee Tavern and Reading Room

Joseph Ferguson began textile manufacture at the Friggate Works in 1824. As his business grew, these works proved inadequate, and he moved to a new factory at Holme Head in 1828. A second mill was opened in 1865 and by 1881, a recreation ground and bowling green had been laid out with a coffee tavern and reading room opened in 1882. The reading room and coffee tavern were built by George Dale Oliver for work people from Fergusons. It stands at the end of Bridge Terrace, a row of terraced houses built by the firm of spinners, weavers, bleachers, printers and finishers in 1852. The gardens in front of the Grade II listed houses were once home to the company's bowling green.

The adjacent large, detached house was once the home of Ferguson Brothers' works manager. The bay opposite was built in 1864 to regulate the flow of water into the mill race, which the factory used both as a source of power and in some of its production processes. In 1947, a British Industries Fair Advert indicated the presence of 'Fabrics, Spinners, Weavers, Bleachers, dyers, Printers and Finishers. Rayon Dress Fabrics, Screen Printed Dress Fabrics, Cotton Dress Fabrics, Lingerie Fabrics, Children's Fabrics, Ladies' Linings and Tailors' Linings'. The factory, later run by CoatsViyella, closed in 1991 with the loss of 200 textile jobs. Today, most of the factory buildings have been redeveloped for housing.

The former Holme Head Works, restored and now residential.

Left: The former home of the work's manager at Holme Head.

Below left: The former reading room and coffee tavern on the corner of North Street, Denton Holme.

Below right: 'Ferguson Brothers Ltd – Registered Office', a reminder of its former history.

Bridge Terrace and the former reading room and coffee tavern. The adjacent bowling green has long since disappeared and is now a community garden.

20. Shaddon Mill and Dixon's Chimney

The first textile factory opened in Carlisle in 1724, but restrictive laws at the time favoured wool and the fact that cotton cloth had to contain a percentage of wool limited what could be made from it. Linen was also produced in the city from 1763, but restrictions on the woven width made it unsuitable for making garments. By 1774 the laws were relaxed and for the first time pure cotton fabrics could be manufactured. The bleaching qualities of the hard water of the River Caldew were an important consideration in the growth of the cotton industry in Carlisle before chemical bleaches were developed in the nineteenth century. The factories were initially concerned with spinning and finishing cloth: all weaving was done by handloom weavers who worked at home, receiving thread from the factory and sending back the lengths of cloth. The cheap cotton fabrics produced were suitable for warm climates and were exported in vast quantities until Carlisle became the fourth most important producing area in the country. One of the finest remnants of this industry today is Shaddon Mill on Shaddongate.

This mill and chimney were constructed in 1836 by Peter Dixon and designed by Mancunian architect Richard Tattersall. The chimney was built to be tall enough to prevent the large amounts of smoke generated by the factory becoming noxious to the rest of the city. In its day, Shaddon Mill was the largest cotton mill in England and had the eighth largest chimney in the world. At its height of production, Peter Dixon & Sons Ltd provided work for 8,000 people in their four mills in the area. A slump in the 1860s was caused by a lack of raw cotton during the American Civil War.

In 1883, Peter Dixon & Sons Ltd went into liquidation and the mill was taken over by Robert Todd & Sons Ltd, who then used the mill for wool production rather than cotton. Expertise of the workpeople in the textile trades attracted many new industries in the city and the industry flourished well into the twentieth century, producing such diverse goods such as curtain fabrics, stockings, felt hats, carpets, and car-seat fabric.

One of the most popular landmarks in the city, seen from miles around.

Above: Restored and now apartments.

Right: An icon of Carlisle – Dixon's Chimney.

The chimney was eventually restored by Carlisle City Council in 1999. Originally it was 305 feet (93 m) tall, but in 1950 it was shortened to 290 feet (88 m). The internal diameter of the chimney remains 17 feet 6 inches (5.33 m) and 10 feet (3.0 m) walls at the base. In 2005 part of the mill was converted into apartments by Story Homes and the other part is used by the University of Cumbria.

21. Cumberland Infirmary and Former Carlisle Dispensary

Medicine and doctors were available in medieval Carlisle but their effectiveness was limited by a lack of knowledge. It was not until 1782 that the Carlisle Dispensary was established (originally in the Tithe Barn and moved to Chapel Street in 1857), which offered the poor free advice and medicine, from doctors who would normally only treat the better-off. Instrumental in setting this up was John Heysham, who as a young doctor in the city kept meticulous records, which, when published as the Bills of Mortality, were used by life insurers nationally to estimate life expectancy. Heysham Park on the Raffles Estate is named after him.

At first, a House of Recovery (or Fever House) was built in 1820 to help in restricting the spread of infectious diseases. This was soon followed by the construction of the Cumberland Infirmary. The original Cumberland Infirmary is a Grade II* listed building, which was designed by Richard Tattersall and constructed by Messrs Robinson and Bennet, contractors from Preston between 1830 and 1832. It actually took until 1841 before it opened because of a dispute with the contractor and was paid for by public subscription. It was soon expanded as Carlisle grew in size and a new wing was opened by the Countess of Lonsdale in October 1911. The founder of the Roper-Logan-Tierney nursing process, Nancy Roper, worked as senior nurse tutor at the hospital in the 1950s. A further extension was opened by Princess Anne in 1975.

The present and modern-day Cumberland Infirmary was procured under a Private Finance Initiative contract in 1997, the first hospital to be bond financed.

The former Carlisle Dispensary on Chapel Street.

The main infirmary building, which opened in 1841.

Health Management (Carlisle) plc, a 50/50 dedicated joint venture company formed by AMEC and Interserve (Facilities Management) Ltd was given a forty-five-year concession period. The hospital, which was built by AMEC, cost £65 million to construct.

Consolidating the operations of three previous hospitals, namely the previous Cumberland Infirmary, the Carlisle City General Hospital and the Carlisle City Maternity Hospital, the Cumberland Infirmary eventually provided 444 beds for the local community. The hospital was officially opened by British Prime Minister Tony Blair on 16 June 2000.

The nearby Crozier Lodge in the grounds of the Infirmary dates back to the late 1820s, and has a uniquely grand feel to it thanks to features such as Venetian windows across all wings, and a central doorway flanked by engaged columns. It was the residence of Thomas McAdam in 1828, and later become the House of Recovery in 1847 and eventually became the doctor's residence for the hospital.

22. The Former Garlands Hospital

Despite early plans to provide an 'asylum' for Cumberland, both that county and neighbouring Westmorland became the last to provide an asylum to comply with the 1845 Act. Although a site had been purchased previously, it was later deemed unsuitable and resold in favour of the Garlands estate near Carleton.

The two counties united for the construction of the asylum, funded according to the anticipated share of accommodation each county needed. J. A. Cory, the county architect, designed an asylum for 200 inmates following a plan created in 1853 by Thomas Worthington and was known as the Cumberland and Westmorland Lunatic Asylum. This had originally been prepared for a separate scheme for a location near Manchester, which was not implemented. Worthington was associated with social reformers such as Mrs Elizabeth Gaskell, the novelist, and whenever possible he sought to secure 'social' commissions, such as hospitals and workhouses. His pioneering hospital design won the praise of no less a figure than Florence Nightingale.

The main building was comprised of an administrative block incorporating medical officer's accommodation, kitchen, laundry, centrally sited water tower and other essential services, three-storey accommodation blocks with a south-west aspect, integral chapel and dining halls and a lodge was located on the main entrance drive to the west. The buildings were constructed in red brick with shallow-pitched slate roofs, with principal buildings bearing distinctive polychromatic banding.

Alterations and additions during the 1870s led to the construction of a detached chapel, opened in 1875, capable of seating 400 persons, followed by a mortuary chapel nearby. A residence for the superintendent was provided in 1878, to the east of the main building. Further additions included two large chronic blocks located either side of the administrative building completed in 1883. The original estate farm was replaced by new facilities in 1888 and a new gas works and water pumping station were built to the north of the main drive in 1888 to provide for the asylum. Further inmate accommodation was added in 1896–97 with the construction of an isolation hospital and two villas for male and female private patients, named Cumberland and Westmorland houses respectively. In 1905, the main building was extended with two projecting blocks for a total of 150 patients, linked by long corridors to the south facade and incorporating new recreation and dining halls. A new lodge and staff housing were added on the service drive during

The former Garlands hospital blocks, now residential.

the 1920s. The superintendent's residence was later altered and extended to form a nurse's home.

Plans for the development of an admissions hospital were shelved during the Second World War, finally being implemented under the NHS and completed in 1962. This area later developed as the Carleton clinic and with the closure of the main building during the 1990s became the focus of remaining services on the Garlands site. With the relocation of the final wards to new premises, the remainder of Garlands hospital was redesignated under the Carlton clinic name.

Following closure of the main building, much of the area to the east of the site was sold for housing development, which occupies the sites of the waterworks, gasworks, adjacent farmland to the north and original patient's blocks. The lodge, administration block, chapel, mortuary, estates buildings and 1905 blocks have survived and are now converted to form private housing. The former superintendent's residence and isolation hospital are currently empty

The former chapel at the Garlands, now converted into residential use.

Former blocks at the Garlands – empty and disused.

and disused. New health service buildings have been erected to the north-west of the admission hospital.

Recent studies of the archives have unearthed full records of all the patients that received treatment at the Garlands, ranging from children as young as four to those in their eighties.

23. The Former County and Station Hotel

On leaving the Citadel railway station, one cannot help but being overwhelmed by the surrounding architecture: there's the Citadel, forming a magnificent gateway to the city, and to the right is a grand hotel. It was originally built as the County and Station Hotel in 1852 by renowned architect Anthony Salvin, with a later extension by Cory and Ferguson of Carlisle. Salvin, who was originally from Sunderland and attended Durham School, was one of the leading architects of the day and was responsible for refurbishing Windsor Castle for Queen Victoria. The *Carlisle Journal* of 20 December 1851 records: 'The building of the new hotel in Court Square has this week been let by tender to Mr Robinson of Penrith.' The cost of the hotel was £11,900. A suite of royal apartments was incorporated into the hotel so that Queen Victoria could stay there; she was to visit for a meal in 1853 but sadly never stayed overnight. Inscribed on pediments are the initials 'G.H.H.', a reference to George Head Head, the well-known Carlisle banker. After several name changes, including the Cumbrian Hotel, the Cumbrian Victorian Hotel, the Lakes Court Hotel, it is now the Hallmark Hotel.

The former County Hotel. (Courtesy of The Carlisle Kid under Creative Commons 2.0)

The Howard Arms and its beautiful tile work advertising its wares for sale.

24. The Howard Arms

The Howard Arms has been registered in local directories since 1855. The exterior Royal Doulton tiles were added around 1895, but when State Management took over in 1916 they were boarded up due to rules preventing advertising outside pubs. The tiles remained hidden until 1979. The interior is a good example of old State Management pubs, with small snug-like rooms and a central bar. It remains one of the most popular public houses in Carlisle.

25. Carlisle Citadel Railway Station

Simon Jenkins includes Carlisle Citadel railway station in his 2017 book, *Britain's 100 Best Railway Stations*. The station was built in 1847, in a neo-Tudor style to the designs of William Tite. It was then one of a number of stations in the city – the others were at Crown Street (Maryport & Carlisle Railway) and London Road (Newcastle and Carlisle Railway) – but had become the main one by 1851. It was expanded and extended in 1875–76 with the arrival of the Midland Railway, which became the seventh different company to serve it.

The Beeching Axe saw two significant rail closures, including the former North British Railway lines to Silloth (closed on 7 September 1964) and Edinburgh via Galashiels (the Waverley Line, closed on 6 January 1969). The closure programme also claimed the Castle Douglas & Dumfries Railway and Portpatrick Railway (the 'Port Road') in 1965, resulting in a significant mileage increase via the Glasgow South Western Line and Ayr to reach Stranraer Harbour and thus Northern Ireland.

The layout has undergone few changes of any significance other than the singling of the ex-NER Tyne Valley route down to London Road Junction as part of the 1972–73 re-signalling scheme associated with West Coast Main Line electrification.

William Tite was a distinguished architect whose railway buildings stretched from Southampton to Perth. Here in Carlisle, he took his theme from the

Citadel Station, Carlisle.

Left: Citadel station from the Courts.

Below: Carlisle Citadel railway station, recognised as one of the best in the country.

adjacent Tudor citadel. Jenkins concludes that 'it has a peculiar sense of grandeur, which seems to derive from Tite's talent in fusing medieval architecture to nineteenth-century engineering'. Pevsner is more effusive, describing as embodying the romance of the northern railway, 'especially on a winter's night when rain-streaked trains rumble in from the outer darkness, pause briefly in the great lighted room and, after a short space, vanish out of sight'.

Right: The architect here was William Tite, who designed many railway stations across the country. (Courtesy of 'Pensioner' Percy)

Below: Wonderful engineering, functional but also fanciful.

26. Congregational Church, Lowther Street

Lowther Street Congregational Church opened on 19 March 1843. The building was designed by architect John Nichol of Edinburgh and Carlisle and constructed with calciferous sandstone ashlar with panelled pilaster quoins carried up as turrets under shaped scrolled pediments and speared ball finials.

A wall-mounted plaque to the exterior refers to Revd Thomas Woodrow, who was minister of this church (on another site) from 1820 to 1835, which was placed to commemorate the visit of his grandson, US President Woodrow Wilson, on 29 December 1918.

The Congregational Church on Lowther Street.

27. St Michael's Church, Stanwix

There has been a succession of churches on this site for at least 1,000 years, but there is archaeological evidence of Christian worship dating back to the early years of the Roman occupation. The World Heritage Site of Hadrian's Wall runs through the parish, though there are no visible traces of the wall or the fort today. One reason for this is probably that most of the masonry was taken to construct other buildings, including the church.

The present church was erected in 1841 to accommodate the growing population of the parish. It is a Grade II listed building in sandstone, with some interesting stained glass commemorating the Roman history of the area. The churchyard contains some interesting items of stonemasonry from previous buildings, and a number of memorials from the time when it was used for burials. One of the most significant is the memorial to the five daughters of Archibald Tait who died within five weeks of one another in 1856. Tait was Dean of Carlisle and went on to be Bishop of London and then Archbishop of Canterbury. Part of the churchyard is now managed as a wildlife area.

The magnificent tower of
St Michael's Church, Stanwix.

28. HSBC and Barclays Banks, English Street

Industry developed in Carlisle and as a result the need for banking grew. Wakefield & Co. Bank was the first bank established in the city. By 1811 there were five banks, all owned privately. A number of these though were badly managed and towards the end of 1836, commercial bankruptcies had caused panic among Carlisle's financiers. Such was the run on Foster's Bank that it had to suspend payments. The crisis was so severe that all of Carlisle's banks folded, with the exception of George Head Head's Bank. George Head Head was Carlisle's most successful banker. His father, Joseph Monkhouse Head, had started a bank in his grocer's shop at the top of Botchergate, which George replaced with the first purpose-built bank in the city. This was demolished in 1865 to make way for what became the Whitehaven-based Cumberland Union Banking Company and eventually was to become a Midland Bank. It is now The Griffin public house.

Head's bank subsequently became London City and Midland Bank (now HSBC). The building seen today is located on the corner of English Street and was built in 1849 by architect T. J. Cox, initially for the Carlisle & District Banking Co., consisting of the full length of the Bank Street façade, which includes the

Once the Cumberland Union Banking Company but also the site of the city's first bank.

Above: Barclays Bank on the corner of English Street.

Right: Barclays Bank, with the beautiful HSBC Bank opposite.

Above: HSBC Bank on the corner of English Street.

Left: Looking up and above and some of the finest architecture in the city is evident.

former manager's house, but just the first two bays to the left of the entrance on English Street. This was all refaced in 1898 by architect T. Taylor-Scott when the canted corner bay was created, along with the ground-floor colonnade. The two further bays on English Street were added in 1920 by the same architect.

Opposite Cox's building was yet another bank. When the Royal Hotel on English Street closed, the premises were also taken over by the Cumberland Union Bank. They left in 1865 and the Carlisle and Cumberland Bank took over the building, which was built in 1875 and today is occupied by Barclays Bank.

29. Former Union Workhouse and City Maternity Hospital, Fusehill Street

Since 1863, these buildings on Fusehill Street had been in use as the Carlisle Union Workhouse. The building of the workhouse was commissioned by the Carlisle Poor Law Union in response to overcrowding at the other workhouses in the city. The main building housed almost 500 inmates. The smaller building on the site was used as an infirmary. It was designed by the architects Lockwood and Mawson, who were responsible for many famous buildings in Bradford, including St George's Hall, Bradford City Hall and also the Wool Exchange.

In April 1916, it was recognised that there was an increasing need for military hospitals in the North West, as Fazakerley in Liverpool was nearing capacity. The inmates of the workhouse were transferred to nearby facilities and the conversion of the buildings began in October 1917. Fusehill could only provide beds for 400 men, so another 250 beds were installed at Brook Street and Norman Street

The former Carlisle workhouse, now a different kind of workplace, and occupied by the University of Cumbria.

Left: Designed by Lockwood and Mawson, architects, who transformed the city of Bradford between 1850 and 1875.

Below: The former Carlisle Maternity Hospital, now occupied by the University of Cumbria.

schools. Unlike auxiliary hospitals in the city, these three sites were managed by the War Office, rather than the Red Cross or the Order of St John.

After the end of the First World War in November 1918, wounded soldiers continued to be treated at Fusehill until it closed in June 1919. The *Carlisle Journal* reported that during its short existence Fusehill War Hospital treated 9,809 patients, and at many times its capacity had reached 861.

Following the war, the buildings returned to their former use as a workhouse and infirmary. In 1938, Fusehill was converted into a municipal hospital, being used a military hospital once more during the Second World War.

With the introduction of the National Health Service in 1948 Fusehill became the City General Hospital, with the infirmary becoming the City Maternity Hospital. The hospital closed in 1999 and the buildings now form part of the Fusehill Campus of the University of Cumbria.

30. Theakston's Carlisle Brewery

The brewery opened in 1756 as Atkinson and Son, and some buildings, although apparently not these, are shown on the City Plan of 1794. The core of the present building is shown on a plan of 1864 in Cumbria County Record Offices. The present buildings were largely erected by Sir Richard Hodgson whose brewery

The former brewery, now occupied by students from all over the country as halls of residence for the University of Cumbria.

The old brewery buildings adjacent to the River Caldew.

it was until nationalisation in 1916 when it became the brewery for the Liquor Control Board, later the Carlisle and District State Management Scheme.

Brewers T&R Theakston Ltd was founded in 1827 by Robert Theakston and John Wood at the Black Bull pub and brewhouse in Masham. By 1832, Theakston had sole ownership of the brewery and in 1875 he passed control over to his son Thomas.

Theakston's expanded into Cumbria in 1974 buying the Carlisle State Management Brewery. The brewery had been owned and operated by the government since 1916. However, the site was a financial drain on Theakston's and led to the company being taken over in 1984 by Blackburn based brewer, Matthew Brown plc. Matthew Brown was itself taken over by Scottish & Newcastle in 1987.

The Carlisle brewery was closed in 1987 and brewing of some Theakston beers was transferred to Scottish & Newcastle's Tyne Brewery. The building has since been converted into flats and accommodation for the University of Cumbria.

31. Viaduct House, Victoria Viaduct

Once occupied by the National Westminster Bank, the building on the corner of the Victoria Viaduct and English Street was built as the reconstructed Bush Hotel in 1877 (dated on the upper stonework). The new hotel was built by architect C. J. Ferguson, with a ground-floor shop, for James Watt of the once highly successful firm of seed merchants, Little and Ballantyne. Originally English Street had run uninterrupted across what is today the entrance to the viaduct. When the viaduct was built English Street was broken through by the demolition of the Old Bush Hotel to form access to the new road and bridge. Blackfriars Street is so called as it leads to the Blackfriars Convent. Chapman's furniture shop was on the site of the old Bush Hotel's stables. Originally Carrs Bread & Flour Co. shop, this building dates to 1878. Cartmell Shepherd's Solicitors now occupy most of the building.

Above: A former bank as well as a hotel, now Viaduct House, is occupied by one of the most well-known solicitors in Carlisle.

Right: Viaduct House is one of Carlisle's 'standout' buildings.

32. The Market Hall and Covered Market

One of the most popular buildings in the city is the Covered Market, also known as the Market Hall. The current building dates back to 1889; however, the beginnings of this building date back to the late eighteenth century. An angry mob of citizens attacked and demolished the Butchers' Shambles in the Market Place in 1788 to protest at the appalling state of the structure. The Corporation was left with a significant problem. It was eventually resolved in 1799 by the purchase of property in Old Blue Bell Lane, between Scotch Street and Fisher Street, where stalls were fitted up for the butchers. The fish merchants, who had also used the Shambles, had to wait a little longer, until 1834, when part of the former Guardhouse in the Market Place was converted into the Fish Market.

A number of extensions were made to the Butcher's Market in 1854 to provide covered accommodation for butter and egg stalls, and a number of the existing stalls were converted for the sale of fish. Further extensions were made in 1879 with an additional entrance at Captain Cook's Lane. The most significant development though was to start in 1887, with the purchase of the adjoining house and gardens, which formerly belonged to the Earl of Lonsdale, which allowed for the new larger Covered Market. The old market was demolished and a new street, Market Street, was laid out and by 1889. The building was completed to the designs of Cawston & Graham, with ironwork manufactured by Cowans, Sheldon & Co. A separate Fish Market was included, as was a Market Arcade and a Coffee Tavern. A Poultry Market also formed yet another extension on West Tower Street in 1900 and part of the interior was divided off to become the Market Hall in the 1960s. The Market Hall became a popular music venue and bands to appear here included a plethora of rock giants including Thin Lizzy, AC/DC, Motörhead, Genesis, Iron Maiden, Gillan, Uriah Heep, The Who and Status Quo.

The Market Hall and former Covered Market. (© Ben Abel)

Above left: Once a popular concert venue, now retail. (© Ben Abel)

Above right: The main entrance from Scotch Street.

The market was redeveloped in the 1990s with the number of stalls reduced and one of the two entrances to Scotch Street closed off. The stalls are now located in the northern half (facing West Tower Street) of the hall while the rest of the building (facing Fisher Street) was at first converted into an arcade of small retail units that were never fully occupied and were then replaced with a branch of Wilko on the ground floor and TK Maxx above.

33. Church of Our Lady and St Joseph, Warwick Square and St Bede's, Wigton Road

Church of Our Lady and St Joseph

In 1798, a Roman Catholic chapel was founded in Carlisle by the Fairburn family on the West Walls. In 1800, a Catholic mission started, supported by the local community. The priest was Joseph Marshall. In the 1820s, with the Catholic population of the city increasing, plans were drawn up to build a church. From 1824 to 1825, one was built on Chapel Street. By the 1870s, this also became too small for the growing congregation, so in 1879 a larger church was planned.

The foundation stone was laid on 18 May 1891. In 1893, the church was opened. The site of the church, Warwick Square, was owned by the Duke of

Left: Our Lady and St Joseph. (© Ben Abel)

Below: The view from Warwick Square.

Devonshire. At the time, the cost of building the church came to £12,000. The church was designed by Dunn, Hansom and Dunn. Archibald Matthias Dunn, his son Archibald Manuel Dunn and Edward Joseph Hansom also designed Our Lady and the English Martyrs Church in Cambridge.

On 15 February 2014, the church, together with Our Lady and St Wilfrid's Church, Warwick Bridge and St Ninian's Chapel in Brampton merged to become Our Lady of Eden Parish. That day, Michael Campbell, Bishop of Lancaster, made Our Lady and St Joseph's a collegiate church, by inviting the Canons of St Ambrose and St Charles Borromeo to serve the parish.

St Bede's Church

On the other side of the town is another Catholic church, completely different in character and style to Our Lady and St Joseph. By 1866, Fr Luke Curry was rector at the Catholic Church of St Mary's and St Joseph's, which had been established in Chapel Street. He founded a mission school at the junction of Wigton Road and Silloth Street. This mission school was dedicated to St Bede.

After eleven years being served from St Mary's and St Joseph's, the parish of St Bedes was established. A new larger school was built on Silloth Street and the original mission school was enlarged to make a permanent church. In the 1930s it became evident that neither the church nor the school were big enough to meet the needs of the parish. Fr Parker bought the land on Wigton Road for this

St Bede's Church, built in 1959.

St Bede's Tower, almost Venetian in design.

magnificent new church and school. However, it was Fr Tootell who was parish priest from 1943 to 1958, who organised the raising of funds to build this new church and school. The new church was built and consecrated in 1959.

34. Hudson Scotts, Carlisle Enterprise Centre and the former Electric Lighting Station Building

Another name still associated with the history of Carlisle is that of Hudson Scott. It was Benjamin Scott who opened a printing and stationery business in English Street in 1799. He retired in 1832 and it was his nephew, Hudson Scott, who took over the business and began printing in colour, using a steam engine to power his presses. His business became incredibly successful and as a consequence he built a factory on James Street in 1869 for Hudson Scott & Sons. This was specifically for stencil printing onto the increasingly popular tin boxes. By 1882, the company had expanded further and employed 200 people. Offset lithography was introduced in 1886 and the production of tin boxes grew substantially. By 1906 there were 1,200 employees and Hudson Scott was the largest metal box manufacturer in the country.

The group continued to expand with a branch factory opening in Newcastle in 1910, a Paris office in 1911 followed by a factory in Workington. By 1921, the company had merged with a number of others and became the Metal Box &

Printing Company, with the Carlisle factory the biggest in the group. The director of Hudson Scott's, F. N. Hepworth, became the first chairman of the Metal Box Company and resisted all efforts to have the company relocate to London. Demand was such that Metal Box had factories all over the world.

In Carlisle, with increased demand, a new can-making plant was built in Botcherby in the mid-1950s. Eventually a takeover by French company, Carnaud was superceded in 1996 when the Crown acquired CarnaudMetalbox and was to become Europe's leading manufacturer of metal and plastic packaging, and becomes the world's packaging leader.

Further up James Street is the former Electric Lighting Station building, also built by Laings in 1899 and opened by the mayor, George White, to supply electricity for domestic and street lighting. Much of the power generated went to power the City of Carlisle Electric Tramway system. The original inscription and coat of arms of the city are still visible on the building. As Carlisle expanded and the number of electricity users increased, a new power station was built at Willow Holme in 1925. Today the building is used as an Enterprise Centre.

The former Electric Lighting Station building, built by Laings in 1899.

Carlisle Electric Lighting Station, now a busy enterprise centre.

Carlisle Enterprise Centre, looking from the River Caldew.

Above: The former Hudson Scott building on James Street, looking for a new purpose.

Left: A reminder of a once great industry.

35. Carlisle Christian Fellowship, Charlotte Street

One of the more unusual buildings in Carlisle is the former Congregational Church on Charlotte Street. Its foundation stone gives a date of 30 April 1860. The architect was Ralph Nicholson, who was based in Halifax and was responsible for a small number of churches in West Yorkshire. He was also responsible for the extension, again dated on the foundation stone as 5 August 1878. Gothic in style, it is built of calciferous sandstone with flush quoins and flying buttresses.

McCarthy (1993) describes life in nineteenth-century Carlisle as 'not easy, despite the growing opportunities and better transport facilities'. Employers such as Laing, Carr and Hudson Scott all ran their businesses on religious principles, heavily influenced by the Quakers, and later by the Brethren. By the mid- to late nineteenth century Nonconformist religious groups had proliferated and were attracting all sections of society; however, internal disputes were frequent and led to many leaving including the Annetwell Street Congregational Church, which led to new churches in Lowther Street, Cecil Street, and here at Charlotte Street. At these churches, railwaymen, shopkeepers and servants rubbed shoulders with families such as the Blaylocks, the Carrs and Hudson Scotts.

The Congregational Church on Charlotte Street eventually closed and became the local Kingdom Hall for Jehovah's Witnesses, but today is the home of the Carlisle Christian Fellowship.

The Carlisle Christian Fellowship building on Charlotte Street, once the Kingdom Hall for Jehovah's Witnesses.

36. Carliol Building Trinity School

In AD 685, St Cuthbert, Bishop of Lindisfarne, visited Carlisle and founded both a school and a church. For the next 900 years the school continued around the grounds of the cathedral. In 1545, the dean and chapter of Carlisle Cathedral took on responsibility for the school in the Cathedral Close. The cathedral was rededicated to the Holy and Undivided Trinity. The school occupied buildings on West Walls, some of which are part of the diocesan offices to this day.

In 1883, this school became Carlisle Grammar School and moved to Strand Road, into what is now the Carliol Building of the school, built to the designs of Carlisle architect George Dale Oliver. As the movement towards comprehensive

The former Carlisle Grammar School, now Trinity School.

The Carliol Building of the current Trinity School.

The Carliol Building and its imposing entrance.

schools took shape, in 1968 the Grammar School amalgamated with two fine local schools, the Margaret Sewell School (for girls) and the Creighton School (for boys), to become Trinity School – a Church of England comprehensive school. In fact, these two schools had already joined forces by then, and all of the sites were along Strand Road, which the school now occupies.

37. Red Gables

Once the home of William Hudson Scott, the *Carlisle Journal* of 1 May 1885 records the acceptance of the design for this fine Victorian building for exhibition at the Royal Academy; it was also illustrated in *The Building News*.

Red Gables, once the home of William Hudson Scott.

William Hudson Scott died here in 1907. Designed by Carlisle architect George Dale Oliver, it is built in the manner of many buildings by the Victorian era's most renowned architect, Alfred Waterhouse, who was responsible for the Natural History Museum in London, as well as Manchester Town Hall and famously used terracotta decoration, as we see here. On Hudson Scott's death the building was converted to a private school and called Red Gables. The school closed in December 1966 and was eventually converted into flats.

38. St Aidan's Church

St Aidan's is a late example of a Gothic Revival church building by architect C. J. Ferguson. This very large church and its attached church hall were built at the same time, with the church started in 1899 and completed by 1902. The north and south aisle arcades, although pointed in form, are very close to being semicircular. The slender columns and wide spans give a very light feeling to the space they define. The fine timber roof is fully exposed internally. Pairs of decorative collar tie trusses span the nave with radiused infill beneath the tie members. Placing of the trusses in order to concentrate load close to the arcade columns has resulted in bays of unequal width, which is also a visual device used to some effect. Internal furnishings and fittings are all of the period of the original build and no significant alterations have been carried out. There are some finely worked features internally, notably the carved oak pulpit with carved stone base and the carved oak font cover at the west end. The church and hall are built entirely of red sandstone with tooled quoins, window surrounds, copings, etc., and with rock-faced ashlar

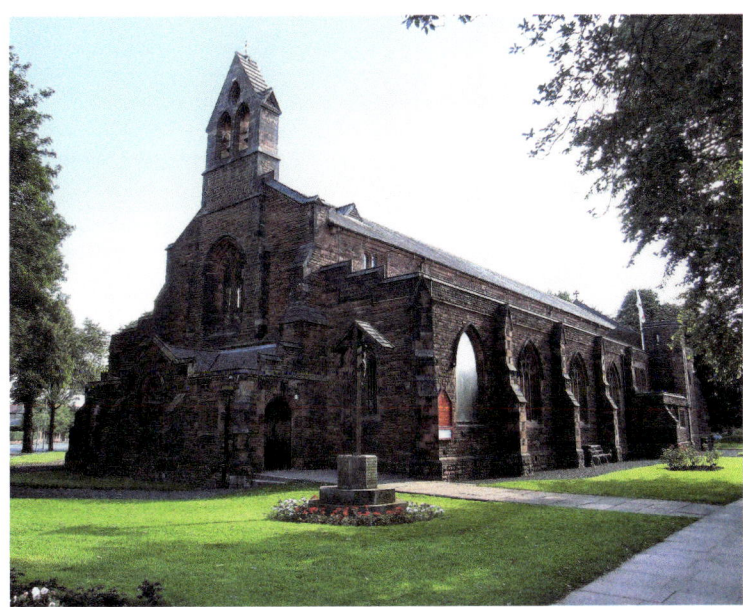

St Aidan's
Church, on
Warwick Road.

walling in narrow courses. Unusually for a church of such size there is no tower or spire. The relatively modest double bell cote comes as something of an anticlimax.

A further inscription on the west wall states: 'The two bells the gift of Mrs Blanshard of Camerton Hall were first rung on 1 January 1900 to usher in the new century.'

39. The Crown and Mitre Hotel

The Crown and Mitre Hotel was built in 1905 on the site of the original Crown and Mitre Coffee House, which had a long and colourful history dating back to before the Jacobite Rebellion. The landlord of the day supported Bonnie Prince Charlie and he gave shelter to the rebels once they entered the city following the Jacobite siege of 1745. By the end of the eighteenth century the Crown and Mitre Coffee House had become the main coaching inn of the city, a stopping place for both mail and stagecoaches on their way to London, Glasgow and Edinburgh.

The Crown and Mitre had a large assembly hall, which once stood on the site of the hotel's ballroom. This assembly hall was the centre of many local activities. A romantic episode of the time was the whirlwind courtship of Miss Margaret Carpenter and Sir Walter Scott, the novelist. They stayed at the Crown and Mitre the night before they were married in the city's cathedral on Christmas Eve.

The original inn was demolished in 1902 to make way for the existing hotel, which took three years to build. No expense was spared during the hotel's construction, all the best materials available were used throughout and when the hotel first opened it was rated as being one of the finest hotels in the north of England. The architect was George Dale Oliver.

George Dale Oliver was born in 1851 at Sunderland, the son of Thomas Oliver, architect, and his wife Elizabeth (née Dale). He was articled to his father in 1867 and in 1871 moved to London to gain wider experience as an improver and latterly assistant in the office of notable architect George Edmund Street. He was subsequently assistant to Joseph Crosby Hetherington in Carlisle, who took him into partnership in 1876. He was awarded the RIBA Silver Medal (Drawings) in 1874. George Dale Oliver continued to practice in Carlisle following the

Above: The Crown and Mitre Hotel – an early view.

Left: Market day in front of the Crown and Mitre.

Above left: The Crown and Mitre Hotel, one of Carlisle's most famous buildings.

Above right: One of architect George Dale Oliver's greatest buildings was the Crown and Mitre hotel here in Carlisle.

dissolution of the partnership with Hetherington, opening a branch office in Workington in 1882. Around 1892 he was appointed county architect for Cumberland, a post that he held until 1919.

Many famous and influential people have visited the Crown and Mitre Hotel. One of the most noteworthy occasions was in 1918 during the state visit to Britain of Woodrow Wilson, president of the United States, President Wilson's mother was born in Carlisle and he called his journey to the city a 'pilgrimage of the heart'.

40. House of Fraser Store

One of the most famous construction companies in the world started in Carlisle. The worldwide empire of Laing plc began here, and by the turn of the twentieth century they had become so well established that in 1907 they built their first department store for Robinson Brothers, who were established in 1889. Their building in Carlisle is much altered from the original, which had a grand arcade and Jacobean café as well as being complete house furnishers and outfitters, and they delivered all their goods free of charge. The shop also expanded back into the former Carlisle Theatre on Blackfriars Street. The brothers also had a shop in Dumfries. Their partnership later dissolved and Frank Robinson took sole charge of the business. He retired in 1933. Binns took over the Carlisle shop in November that year. This Sunderland-based department store chain was absorbed

The House of Fraser store in Carlisle city centre.

into House of Fraser in 1953. When House of Fraser was bought by a consortium in 2006 most Binns stores, including Carlisle's, were renamed House of Fraser. In 2020, many of these once great department stores had uncertain futures with the significant move to online shopping, meaning great changes for the high street.

41. Brunton Park, Warwick Road

Carlisle United's ground was first built on Brunton Park back in 1909 after the club, who were originally known as Shaddongate United, felt that their ground at Millholme Bank was too small to satisfy the local area's demand for live football. After occasionally using the larger rugby ground, and then for a while the facilities at Devonshire Park, the club moved to the current site at Brunton Park after the land's owner, the Duke of Devonshire, asked the club to relocate.

With stands constructed and the club now with a permanent home, it looked like Carlisle United would establish themselves as one of the best teams in England; however, in 1953 they were forced to sell off local player Geoff Twentyman to Liverpool FC for £12,500. This was deemed a necessary evil after the Main

The theatre of dreams for many Cumbrians and the 'Blue Army' – Brunton Park.

Stand was burnt to the ground as a result of an unfortunate electrical fault. This set the club back a good few years in terms of development, and at the start of 2005 disaster struck again when flooding meant the club had to play their home matches at Morecambe's Christie Park for the second half of the season.

With facilities remaining relatively untouched since 1996, when the East Stand was opened at the start of the season, the club have occasionally explored plans to relocate to more modern facilities. The most ambitious of these were presented in the late 1990s by former owner Michael Knighton, who formulated plans for a large 28,000-capacity ground. These are contrasted by a later vision in 2011 of a 12,000-capacity ground in the Kingmoor area of Carlisle known as 'Project Blue Yonder'.

42. Turkish Baths, James Street

Listed in 2020, this set of Edwardian Turkish baths, which were constructed in 1909 by county surveyor W.C. Marks, have been designated for the following principal reasons: Decorative Scheme – the original internal decorative tiling and glazed faience work by the respected company Minton and Hollins of

Stoke, notably in the cool room, is of good quality and complete; Intactness – alterations are few and the original plan of the baths remains intact, which renders the Turkish bathing process highly readable; and Rarity – this building is an increasingly rare example of a once common building form, of which only around twenty remain in England. It compares very favourably with the eight existing listed Turkish Baths.

The first Turkish baths to have been built in the British Isles was in 1857 in Blarney, County Cork, and the first in England was in London in 1860. Subsequently many hundreds were constructed, often as part of publicly funded swimming facilities, although only around twenty examples remain in England today.

Plans for the provision of Turkish baths in Carlisle occurred as early as 1884 when the existing public swimming baths were opened. The idea was resurrected in 1901 and agreed in 1902, although it was a further six years before plans were finally approved. The Turkish baths opened on 20 September 1909 in a purpose-built extension to the existing public baths building at a cost of £2,500. The internal tiling and glazed faience work was by Minton and Hollins Co. of Stoke, one of the leaders in the field of tile manufacture. The opening of the suite was celebrated in the local newspapers, which describes a public inspection in detail, although there was no formal opening. Entry cost between 1 and 2 shillings depending on the time and day of the week and bathing was expected to take around one and a half hours. The Turkish baths remain open and in use to the present time.

Above left: The Turkish Baths look almost like a prison building from the outside, but have an incredible interior.

Above right: The interior of the Turkish Baths.

43. Former Crown Post Office, Warwick Road

The Halston is housed in Warwick Road's former General Post Office, which opened on 27 February 1916. The site was previously Bartons Yard and home to William Barton and his business partner Robert Tweeddale's horse harness and coach manufacturing business, which also supplied horses for mail coaches during the 1830s to 1840s. In the early 1900s, local construction company Laings won the contract to build the post office. It carved the fluted columns and intricate design of the building's neoclassical façade with stone from Blaxter quarries in Northumberland. The building was impressive inside and out, with the horseshoe-shaped public counter on the ground floor made from the finest mahogany.

New Post Office, Carlisle.

Right: What was the new post office on Warwick Road.

Below: Once a post office and now a top hotel, the Halston.

The Warwick Road post office served the people of Carlisle for many years until it was closed in 2008.

Many post offices emanating from the architects of the Office of Works in the period around 1905–18 were of considerable merit and, in terms of the stylistic development of British architecture, highly interesting. Unlike most other types of buildings, the construction of which was halted or at least diminished by the 1914–18 war, post office building activity seemingly continued largely unaffected, in part because of the need to maintain efficient lines of communication. As such, stylistic trends, which were prematurely interrupted in other types of buildings, were allowed full expression, and thus, almost uniquely, post offices provide a rare glimpse into the transition from Edwardian mannerism to interwar classicism as we see here in Carlisle. This continuity and quality of output was doubtless related to the fact that, by the Edwardian period the Office of Works' Architects division comprised well-established, and presumably largely self-contained, divisions specialising in particular building types overseen by the three principal architects for England. The Office of Works Staff List for 1914–15 reveals that by that date the substantial and specialised post office division was headed by Walter Pott, and comprised four regional teams: South-West & Midlands branch (H. A. Collins, head architect); South-East branch and London North & North-West districts (Albert Robert Myers, head architect); London branch (except north and north-west districts; E. Cropper, head architect); and a North branch (Charles P. Wilkinson, head architect). The architect of the Carlisle Post Office was Charles P. Wilkinson.

In 2011 Burge Halston purchased the building with a vision to bring something new and exciting to Carlisle and plans were drawn up for the city's first ever aparthotel – The Halston, its current use.

44. Central Methodist Hall, Fisher Street

Built in 1922 at an estimated cost of £26,000, the Central Methodist Hall in Carlisle eventually closed in 2005. It was opened on 12 April 1923 by Mr Joseph Rank. This former Methodist church occupies a very prominent position on Fisher Street, within walking distance of the Market Hall. It is a striking red sandstone building with a high level of classical detailing. Retained within the interior of the building are some very attractive decorative plasterwork interiors. The building, now listed Grade II, reflects the importance of Nonconformist worship within Carlisle in the early twentieth century.

The church was designed by architects Brocklehurst and Hornabrook and primarily funded with £10,000 from the millionaire philanthropist Joseph Rank (of Hovis bread fame). The remainder of the money was raised by the first minister of the church, Revd Bramwell Evans, who later became a national icon as the

Above and right: The
Central Methodist Hall
on Fisher Street.

voice of BBC Radio's *Romany* – the children's nature programme that inspired
the likes of David Attenborough and David Bellamy. Inside the main building is
a large auditorium with balcony and is suitable for seating and accommodating
around 500 people. It is believed that while the building was occupied by the
Methodists, staff kept a box of real Roman sandals in the office cupboard. These
sandals were found on the site during excavation works. Other ancient relics were
also discovered; these are now in Tullie House Museum.

45. Former Fire and Police Headquarters, Rickergate

The fire and police headquarters on Rickergate was once the site of the former Assembly Rooms, which were built in 1887, and was to become the Star Music Hall. By 1898, the music hall closed to become initially a Salvation Army Citadel, then later a band practice room. The building was demolished in 1938 to make way for the current building, which became the fire and police headquarters in Rickergate. The building, designed by Percy Dalton, city surveyor and engineer 1921–49, was built by Messrs John Laing & Son Ltd.

Built of stone from Greenlaw Quarry in Northumberland, it also included some artificial stone. Cottages were provided for permanent members of the brigade in Warwick Street, which, along with Peter Street, was considerably widened. The *Carlisle Journal* goes on to say that Percy Dalton visited many of the newest fire stations while he was designing the building. Dalton describes the building as 'containing an engine room, which can accommodate six engines and adjoining this is the watch room, which was the nerve centre of the whole. Above on the next floor, was a large recreation room and adjoining this is a reading room … there is also a billiards room upstairs, and the superintendents flat … To save time when the men have to take up their action stations a sliding pole connects the upper floor with the engine room'.

Dalton designed the building long before the Second World War broke out and a number of changes had to be made to meet war conditions. The remainder of the

The old fire station, now an arts centre.

Right: Shades of its former use – the old fire station.

Below: The former police station and current magistrates' courts on Rickergate.

buildings consisted of a police station with approximately 100 rooms devoted to various purposes, including a large courthouse. Between the police and fire station was a small separate block of buildings, the ground floor of which accommodated the Weights and Measures department. The police station itself, was opened in April 1941 and 'marked another epoch in the history of the ancient City of Carlisle'.

After catastrophic storms in 2005 the building was flooded, and the services left in 2012 and in 2015. After the emergency services moved out it was converted into an arts centre in May that year, following a £1 million redevelopment by Carlisle City Council, but was once again subject to major flooding in 2016 as a result of Storm Desmond. By September, it was back in business after repair costs in the region of £500,000.

46. Carlisle Public Houses by Harry Redfern

As chief architect of the State Management Scheme in the interwar years, Harry Redfern was responsible for designing, in an imaginative and varied manner, a number of notable and totally unique public houses in the Carlisle district. The scheme built fourteen exclusive New Model Inns to Redfern's designs in and around Carlisle, using a strong theme of the Arts and Crafts movement.

He was commemorated towards the end of his work by the naming of Redfern Inn (1938) in Etterby, a district of Carlisle. With Redfern's collaboration, The Redfern was actually designed by his assistant architect, Joseph Seddon. It was a tribute to a man who had dedicated his talents to the quest for an improved public house style. Redfern practised from Porchester Gardens, London, but lived in a very simple semi-detached house in Ealing. He died in 1950, leaving Carlisle with a legacy of national heritage.

The Former Albion Hotel (now The Border Rambler)

The original Albion Hotel at Nos 45–47 Botchergate was purpose built as a pub and opened in February 1859. The original entrance was off Portland Place, as there were two shops on the Botchergate frontage. These were demolished in 1905 to enable the pub to be enlarged by the time it was taken over by the State Management Board in August 1916. After they bought it extensive alterations were made and it was closed from October 1916 to enable Redfern to redesign it. His new pub occupied the site of the original Albion together with half the site of the adjoining pub the Deakin's Vaults. The other half of the Vaults was turned into a shop. It reopened on 7 June 1917. The bar was on the ground floor and consisted of a large open room instead of the four small rooms that were in the old pub and provided with seats, tables and chairs. It was always somewhat of a rough pub in the State Management days and was once described as a bit like an eighteenth-century gin house but not that good!

One interesting feature in keeping with the principles behind the State Management philosophy of introducing food into pubs was the opening of the Albion Café upstairs. This dining room was entered by a separate door from the street. It had previously been a billiard room. The facilities available in the dining room apparently took some time to become known, but once known they became very popular.

Another feature of the State Management Scheme was that all employees were civil servants and therefore were eligible for awards like any other civil servant. A Mary Bowie, who retired after almost twenty-eight years' service at the Albion Café, was recommended for the award of the Imperial Service Medal. The recommendation, that had to go to the Home Office for approval, stated that her service 'had been meritorious and her loyalty to the Department had never wavered'.

The Border Rambler on historic Botchergate.

The Cumberland Inn

The original mid-Victorian Cumberland Inn was replaced when the present building was opened on 29 September 1930. It was designed by Redfern and built by J&R Bell of Carlisle. Redfern commemorated the builders with a stained-glass rebus in six of the windows in the mixed first-class bar on the first floor. It is the least altered of all Redfern's designs for the State Management Scheme.

Almost out of place on Botchergate, the Cumberland Inn.

The Former Crescent Inn and Andalusian

This fine Grade II listed former public house was built in 1932 in a Hispano-Moresque style. It is one of the many designed public houses by architect Harry Redfern for the Carlisle and the District State Management Scheme, but this is deemed his most flamboyant of designs. The scheme took pubs and breweries under government control during the First World War to curb excessive drinking by munitions workers, and continued until 1971. The pub closed in January 2007 and became the White House Inn, and is now an Italian restaurant.

The design of this building is very out of keeping with much of the architecture of the time. Redfern's vision for Carlisle pubs first took shape with his reworking of the Malt Shovel on the corner of Corporation Road, with others that followed, including The Apple Tree in Lowther Street, the Coach and Horses in Kingstown, the Magpie in Botcherby, and many others.

One of the more fascinating buildings in Carlisle: the former Crescent Inn and Andalusian.

The Magpie Inn

The Magpie, designed by Redfern and built by John Laings, was opened on 4 December 1933. The city council had bought part of the land belonging to the owner of Botcherby Hall for the widening of Warwick Road/Victoria Road. The scheme agreed to buy 4,278 square yards of land fronting onto Victoria Road and Botcherby Hall (for demolition) and build a new model inn to replace the old Star Inn, which had been the only pub in that part of the city. It had also been a centre for communal and sporting activities.

Redfern's concept was of a black and white magpie house nestling in a hollow formed by two steep grassy banks to make use of 'an uncluttered Arts and Crafts style with subtle asymmetry, half-timbering, horizontal fenestration and a diamond-shaped window'. There was a deep pitch to the gable-ended roof, the hipped roof dormers, and the tall chimney stacks balancing he fenestration. He provided a wide forecourt for a car park and a pergola porch. At the back paved terraces and steps led to the bowling green that became a feature of Redfern's model pubs. The bowling green was fronted by flower beds. Redfern himself chose the shrubs and plants that he wanted and positioned them exactly where he wanted them. The principle being that the internal and external design was one entity. The sloping nature of the site added to the interest of the site, half of which was given over to the bowling green.

Redfern wanted to create a feeling of restfulness inside with a 'quiet' colour scheme. His usual coal fires and the long low line of windows with their height designed to suit the number of brick courses. The fireplaces were of white shawksone briquettes with a selection of blocks slightly veined in red. The toilet accommodation was carefully designed as usual with twin entrance porches for tearoom and smoking room customers. The public bar toilet was accessed internally via a small lobby. This toilet also served the needs of the bowlers with a door from the verandah.

Olive Seabury in her book *The Carlisle State Management Scheme* gives a full description of the rules and regulations that the contractors had to follow to the letter and clearly show how Redfern's words were gospel. Although these rules quoted here refer only to the installation of the electric light wiring and fittings all the work had to follow strict rules.

> The whole of the work to be executed in accordance with the drawings to the entire satisfaction of the architect. Materials and workmanship to be the best of their kind and only skilled labour to be employed. A skilled foreman to be constantly employed during the execution of the work. Any defects which may occur six months after completion of the work must be made good at the contractor's own expense. Payment will be made at the rate of 80% of the value of the work from time to time as the work proceeds and the remainder will be paid at the rate of 10% on completion and 10% three months after completion. The contractor to commence

The Magpie Inn in Arts and Crafts style.

the work immediately on receiving instructions from the architect and complete the whole of the work within six weeks from the date of commencement.

A modification was proposed in 1949 suggesting a glazed verandah erected in such a way that during the bowls season a set of folding doors in the wide centre opening could be opened right back. For the rest of the year, with these doors closed, the verandah could be used as a darts alley and an area could be heated by the installation of two 2-kilowatt heaters. Once the suggestion was agreed with Redfern the work was carried out. The general manager was concerned, however, about how the area could be supervised to prevent gambling during busy times at the weekends. It was decreed then that darts were not to be played except under supervision by the pub's manager, who had to ensure there was no gambling.

The Redfern
Harry Redfern suffered a heart attack in December 1936 and his doctor would not allow him to travel for some time. His wife died in May 1937. Carlisle, however, needed a new pub as a £1 million RAF equipment depot (14 MU) was being built and it was expected to bring about 3,000 workers to the area. Temperance protesters were told that a new pub would be needed to prevent overcrowding at the existing pubs. Joseph Seddon, Redfern's assistant was commissioned to design this new pub. In gratitude for Harry Redfern's work and commitment to Carlisle it was decided to name this pub the Redfern Inn and it was opened on 1 October 1940. It was agreed at the outset that the design must include a bowling green,

The Redfern, named after the architect himself.

and this influenced the design as there was only one position for this green. When Redfern finally saw the pub that bore his name he is quoted as saying: 'I fell in love with the building when I saw it and should be proud to think that I had designed it. But all the kudos for that goes to our good Seddon.'

47. Eden Bridge Gardens Rest Rooms

Visible from the Eden Bridge or from the back of the Sands Leisure Centre are the Eden Bridge Gardens. The significance of these municipal gardens is largely unknown to most of the city's inhabitants. The Eden Bridge Gardens were designed by the internationally renowned landscape architects Thomas H. Mawson & Sons.

These gardens have been known locally for many years as the 'Chinese Gardens' or 'Japanese Gardens', probably because of the rockeries and Japanese maple trees that dominate. However, there is nothing Chinese or Japanese in the design and anybody knowledgeable in the works of Thomas Mawson and his practice will know that he was famed for his grand Italianate garden designs, many of which still exist at many stately homes, including Rydal Hall in Cumbria. Mawson was also famous for a number of public parks including Burslem Park and Hanley Park, both in Stoke-on-Trent.

Built using unemployed labour in the depression of the 1930s, under the supervision of the city engineer, Percy Dalton, these gardens cost just over £3,000, the cost being kept down by the use of reclaimed materials. The white cove stone used to make the two restrooms, one for ladies and one for gentlemen, was taken from the old Eden Bridge parapets that were demolished during the bridge widening operations of 1930 to 1932. The sandstone used to build the retaining

The restrooms of the Eden Bridge Gardens.

walls was taken from the old gaol in English Street and the crazy paving paths that run throughout the garden was taken from the old road, which used to pass over Eden Bridge – all of this long before the concept of 'recycling' was even heard of.

Opened in 1933 by the city mayor, Councillor E. B Gray, the design featured the classic Mawson pergolas and raised terraces overlooking lily ponds. Crazy paving and a simple rock garden complete the setting. Most of the design work is likely to be attributed to Thomas Mawsons' son Edward or Prentice as Thomas was suffering from Parkinson's disease and died in November 1933. This was possibly one of the last designs that Thomas Mawson may have contributed to.

Sadly the gardens fell into disrepair, but a grant of £50,000 from the Heritage Lottery Fund assisted the city council with its ultimate restoration.

48. St Barnabas Church

When the Raffles estate was developed in the 1920s and 1930s, there was no church to serve the area, so St Barnabas Church was built. A particularly delightful modern church of very unusual character, it was designed by John Seely and Paul Paget and built by John Laing and Sons in 1935. As many of the houses had been built by Laings, it made sense to award them the contract. The structure

Almost Mediterranean in style, St Barnabas Church on the Raffles estate.

of the church is reinforced concrete and the principal roof surfaces are of green Westmoreland slate with copper flashings and dormers. The external wall surfaces are of painted render, unlike any other in Carlisle. The church offers a refreshing use of innovating detailing and an integrated design of furnishings and fittings. Original external wall lanterns remain in position although were in need of repair. There is a complete set of contemporary oak furnishings and the elegant linked ranks of seating with folding seats are of particular interest. The oak lectern does not appear to be of the same period. Bold and simple use of stained glass is to be found in the three lancets of the Lady Chapel and the circular window above the altar. This church is a rare and important example in Carlisle of 1930s architecture. The adjacent vicarage was the design of Fawcett Martindale, a Carlisle architect.

49. Civic Centre, Rickergate

One of the most controversial buildings in Carlisle, and remains so to this day, is the iconic Civic Centre on Rickergate. Opened in 1964, it was designed by architects Charles B. Pearson and Partners. This is Carlisle's very own monument to modernist architecture. The architects beat off 200 other companies in the competition to win this commission. Built by Carlisle firm John Laing Construction, it included materials from East African Olive and Brazilian Rose woods and was originally decorated with Finnish lampshades and Japanese silk wallpapers. There was also 37,000 square feet of French white and Italian pink mosaic on the outside cladding, and more electric lamps than in the whole of the city streets. Built at a cost of £820,000, it has been called a grand civic and engineering statement by the Carlisle and District Civic Trust. The building design was 'commended' in the 1966 National Civic Trust Awards. The mid-1960s were an optimistic time with ample funding around to build such grandiose structures for local government.

Above: Carlisle Civic Centre, the seat of local government in the city.

Right: Brutalist in design, the rotunda is a fine example of this style of architecture.

In 2020, the building remained divisive with plans to demolish it, including the rotunda, and replace it with a complex of shopping and restaurants in its place. Yet, the tower is one of the defining landmarks of the city, towering over the city at an impressive 135 feet tall. Plans have been as controversial as the building itself, which has suffered at the hands of repeated floods in recent years. Many have now come forward in defence of the building due to its architectural importance. New York architect Wayne Turett says:

> The point is not whether you like the Carlisle Civic Centre – that kind of personal decision is better left for the colour of your kitchen walls – but that demolishing a building should not be considered lightly. It is a fine example of mid-century modern architecture with an architectural, interior, product and graphic design style that is now recognised by scholars and museums worldwide as a significant design movement.

50. Cumbria County Council Offices, Botchergate

As part of an ongoing cost-saving exercise, Cumbria County Council moved into a new custom-built £10.4 million office block in central Carlisle. By moving the majority of its staff into these new premises, the council was able to sell more than twenty older offices throughout the city. Located on the historic Botchergate, the headquarters building now accommodates around 700 staff. To prepare the site, a number of shops and houses were demolished and pad foundations installed in readiness for the steel frame. An archeological dig was also undertaken during the early part of the programme. Medieval and Roman artifacts were unearthed.

This steel-framed building was configured into two connected parts, consisting of a four-storey office block arranged around a large central atrium and a two-storey element at the front, which contains the public areas and the main entrance. The building was opened in 2016.

The new county council offices in Botchergate, part of the ongoing regeneration of this part of the city.

Bibliography

Carlisle Cathedral (Pitkin Guide, 2000)

Carlisle (Carlisle Corporation, 1957)

Charlton, John, *Carlisle Castle* (English Heritage, 1986)

Constantine, Matthew, *Carlisle: A History & Celebration* (Francis Frith, 2005)

Cumberland News, Images of Carlisle (Breedon Books, 1999)

Davies, Hunter, *Strong Lad Wanted for Strong Lass: Growing Up In Carlisle* (Bookcase, 2004)

Dickens, Marie K., *Changing the Face of Carlisle: The Life and Times of Percy Dalton City Engineer and Surveyor, 1926–1949* (Hayloft, 2002)

Eldridge, Jim, *A Canny History of Carlisle* (Bookcase, 2006)

Emett, Charlie and J. P Templeton, *Carlisle People and Places* (The History Press, 2012)

Kemp, Laurie and Jim Templeton, *175 Years of Carlisle* (Archive Publications, 1990)

McCarthy, Mike, *Carlisle: History and Guide* (Alan Sutton, 1993)

Nelson, Elizabeth, *Around Carlisle* (Sutton Publishing, 1997)

Nutter, M. E., *Carlisle in the Olden Time: A Series Of Views Of Ancient Public Buildings* (Charles Thurnam, 1835)

Perriam, D. R., *Carlisle: An Illustrated History* (Bookcase, 1992)

Perriam, Denis, *Carlisle: From the Kendall Collection* (Tempus, 2002)

Recreation & Amenities Committee, Carlisle City Council, *Carlisle Museum*, Pamphlet

Stables, Andrew Graham, *A–Z of Carlisle: Places-People-History* (Amberley Publishing, 2019)

Templeton, James P., *Old Carlisle: A Second Photographic Recollection* (Dalesman, 1978)

Templeton, James P., *Carlisle: A Photographic Recollection* (Dalesman, 1976)

Acknowledgements

Paul Rabbitts would like to thank the following: all previous colleagues who he worked with while living in Carlisle, but in particular Marie Crabb, Alan Marham, David Nightingale, Elizabeth Allnutt, Andy Bradbury, Steve Crabtree, Rob Burns, Gill Burns, Eddie Edge, Jackie Bell, Sue Oliver, Richard Broadley, Neil Griffiths, Lisa Johnston, Dave Ingham, Steve Carruthers, Jilly Hale, Norman Tolson, Debbie Richardson, Brian Hill, Colin Johnson, Julie Gallagher, Peter Messenger, Euan Cartwright and, of course, the late Chris Wright, who gave me the best job ever.

About the Author

Paul Rabbitts is a Fellow of the Royal Society of Arts and a Fellow of the Landscape Institute. He is currently Head of Parks, Heritage and Culture for Watford Borough Council and is also a prolific author on architecture, public parks and a noted expert on the history of the Victorian and Edwardian bandstand. He has written several books in the 'in 50 Buildings' series, including Watford, Leighton Buzzard, Luton, Salford, Bournemouth, Windsor, Salisbury, Hertford, Welwyn Garden City and Manchester. He is a former resident of Carlisle, having lived there from 1992 to 1999, and was Carlisle City Council's first landscape architect, and while working there designed the extension in Bitts Park, restored Hammonds Pond, one of the first lottery-funded park restorations in the country, and planted many trees across the city, which are looking very fine indeed.